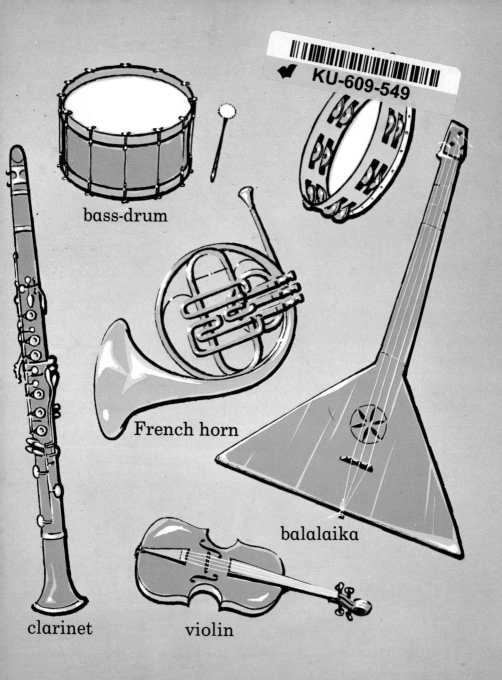

bass-drum

French horn

balalaika

clarinet

violin

First Published in 1970 by
Macdonald and Company
(Publishers) Limited
St. Giles House
49-50 Poland Street
London W1

Managing Editor
Michael W. Dempsey B.A.
Chief Editor
Angela Sheehan B.A.

Made and printed in Great Britain
by A. Wheaton & Company
Exeter Devon

MACDONALD FIRST LIBRARY

Sounds and Music

Macdonald Educational
49-50 Poland Street
London W1

There are sounds about
us all the time.

We hear the sounds of
cars, trains, and
aircraft.

We hear the sound of
bird-song and music.

There are many different
sounds.

Some are loud and noisy.

Some are soft and
peaceful.

If you throw a stone into a pond, you will see small waves, or ripples, spreading out over the water.

The same kind of thing happens when you hit a gong.

waves

gong

You cannot see the waves that spread out when you hit a gong, but you can hear them. They are sound waves.

Sounds are made when something shakes, or vibrates.

If you stretch a rubber-band and then pluck
it, you will see it move backwards and
forwards.
This movement is called vibration.

You will also hear a sound.
The sound comes from the vibration.

If you stretch the rubber-band even more and
then pluck it, it will vibrate faster.
It will make a higher sound.
The faster the vibrations, the higher the
sound.

We call the highness or lowness of a sound,
its pitch.

The best way to make a
band, or string, vibrate
faster or slower is to
change its length and
thickness.

Short, tight strings make
higher notes.
Long, loose strings make
lower notes.

You can see how this
works on the harp and
on the piano.
The harp has 45 strings.
Each one is a different
length and thickness.

harp

The piano also has strings of different
length and thickness.

The strings vibrate when they are hit
by a small hammer.
To make the hammer hit its string, the
player presses down a key.

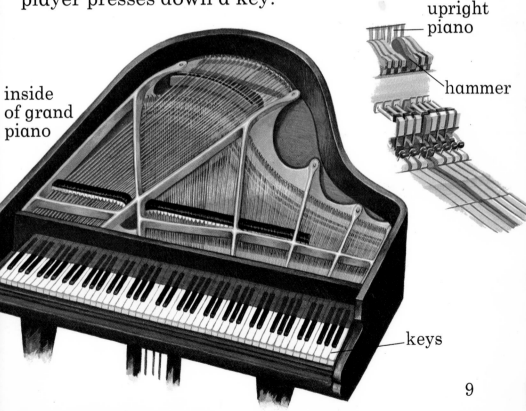

strings of
upright
piano

hammer

inside
of grand
piano

keys

9

The piano is a keyboard instrument.

The harpsichord and the spinet are also keyboard instruments.

They were invented long before the piano.

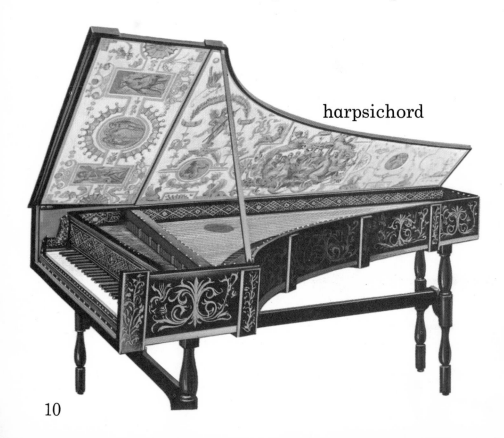

harpsichord

spinet

They have strings of different lengths just like the piano.

But the keys are not hit by hammers.

They are plucked by little hooks, called jacks.

guitar

Having a different string for each note takes up a lot of room.

A guitar does not take up much room.

It has only six strings.

The guitar player presses on the strings to change their length.
This changes the pitch of the note.

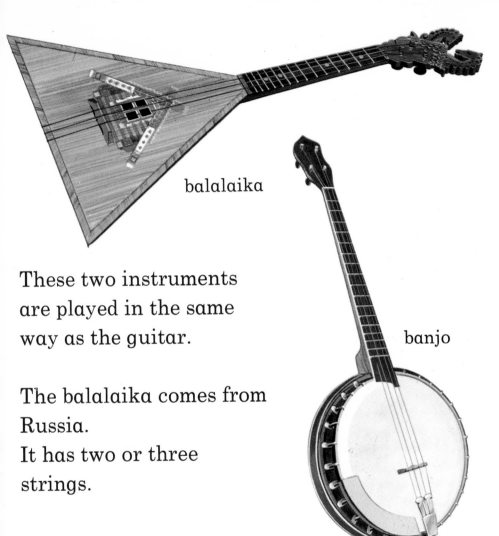

balalaika

banjo

These two instruments
are played in the same
way as the guitar.

The balalaika comes from
Russia.
It has two or three
strings.

The banjo usually has
four or five strings.

The violin is a stringed instrument.

violin

It has four strings.
Each one is a different thickness.
The player draws a bow across the strings to make them vibrate.

The violin is quite small, so its strings are not very long.
This means that none of its notes is very low.
The player can press the strings to make the pitch higher.

The 'cello has longer
strings, so its notes
are lower.
The strings of the
double-bass are even
longer, so it can play
even lower notes.

double-bass

'cello

Alpine horn

Not all musical instruments have strings.
Some have pipes.
There are many different kinds of pipes and
they are played in different ways.
This pipe is an Alpine horn.

flute

If you hold the mouth of
a bottle to your lips
and blow across it, you
can make a sound come
from the bottle.
The sound comes from air
vibrating in the bottle.

If you put water in
the bottle, there will
be less air to vibrate.
The note will be higher.

If you look at a flute
player, you will see
that he blows across the
mouth of the flute in
the same way.

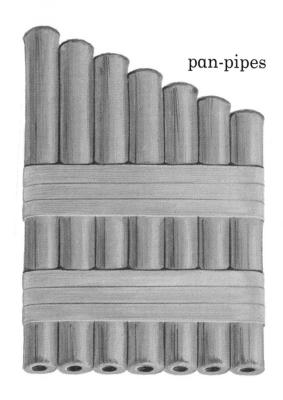

pan-pipes

If a pipe is short the note is high.
If a pipe is long the note is low.
In the pan-pipes, each pipe is a different
length.
The pipes are like the strings on a harp.
Each one plays a different note.

The pan-pipes were named after Pan, the Greek god of Nature.
Pan was half-man and half-beast.

It is said that the music he played on his pipes was so sweet that all the animals came to listen.

recorder

Most wind instruments
have only one pipe.
There are small holes
in the side of the pipe.
The player can cover the
holes with his fingers.
This makes the pipe
'longer'.

The recorder is played
like this.
The air vibrates inside
the pipe to make a
sound.
If the holes are not
covered the note will
be higher because the
pipe is 'shorter'.

holes
open
higher
pitch

holes
covered
lower
pitch

pipe

air

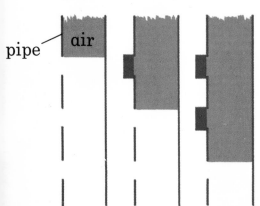

All these instruments are woodwind
instruments.

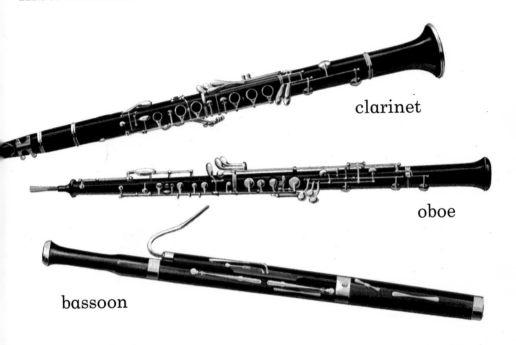

clarinet

oboe

bassoon

Most woodwind instruments have little strips
of wood which vibrate when the player blows
on them.
These strips of wood are called reeds.

trombone

In other wind instruments, the player moves
his lips to make the sound.

Some of these instruments have valves which
cut off parts of the tube or pipe.

This makes the tube longer or shorter.

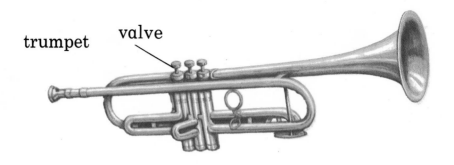

trumpet   valve

French horn

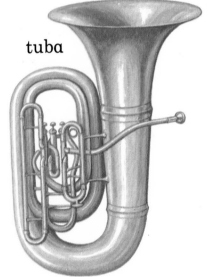

tuba

The tubes of some
instruments are so long
that they need to be
coiled round themselves.
They would be very
long indeed if they were
not coiled.
These are all brass
instruments.

bagpipes

There are other
instruments that have
wind blown through them.
In the bagpipes the
player blows into a sack.
He presses the sack with
his elbow to force the
air into the pipes.
The accordion player
moves the accordion in
and out, like bellows, to
force air in and out.

accordion

organ

The organ has many pipes.
Nobody could blow hard enough to make an organ play.
The organ has a pump to blow the air into the pipes.

Some instruments are hit to make them
vibrate.

They are called percussion instruments.

The xylophone is a percussion instrument.

The xylophone has many wooden bars.

The longer bars make lower notes.

The shorter bars make higher notes.

xylophone

triangle

drum

tambourine

cymbals

Here are some more percussion instruments.
Drums have skins stretched tightly across a
frame.
The skin vibrates when the drum is hit.
Large drums make lower notes than small ones.

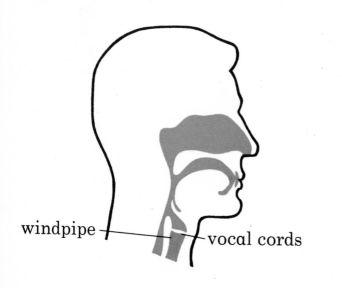

windpipe —————— vocal cords

vocal
cords
loose

vocal
cords
tight

Our own voices are a kind of musical
instrument.

There is a voice box inside our throats.

There are two thick cords inside the voice
box.

They are called vocal cords.

The air from our lungs makes the vocal
cords vibrate.

When we speak or sing we stretch or loosen
the cords to make higher or lower sounds.

By using many instruments together we can make wonderful sounds.
In the orchestra there are stringed, woodwind, brass and percussion instruments.

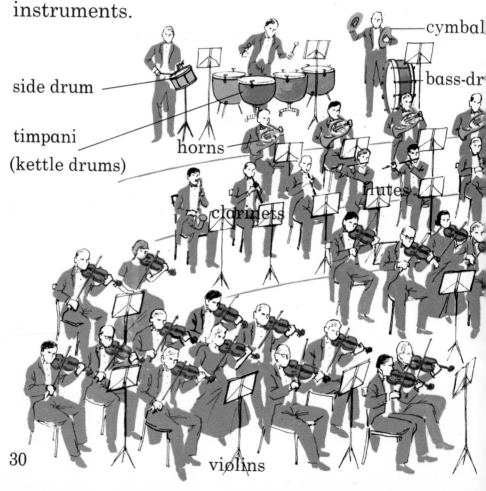

cymbal

side drum

bass-dr

timpani
(kettle drums)

horns

flutes

clarinets

violins

Before a concert the conductor tells the
players how best to play the music.
At the concert, he keeps time and guides
them by waving his baton.

tuba

trombones

double-basses

trumpets

oes   bassoons

harp

violas

conductor

'cellos

Index

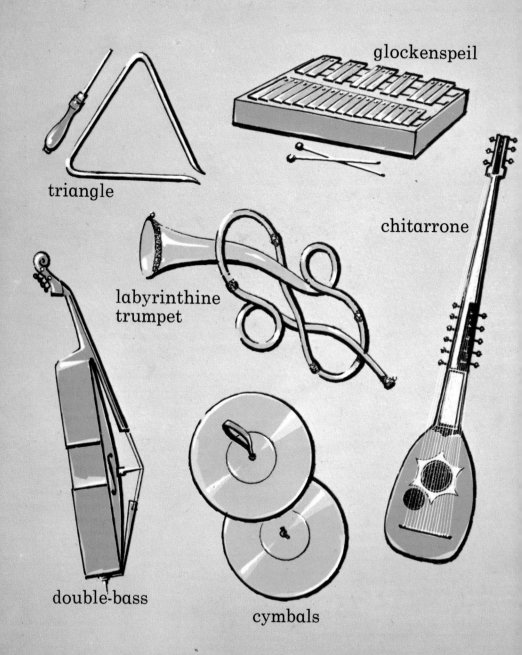

triangle

glockenspeil

chitarrone

labyrinthine
trumpet

double-bass

cymbals